Organic Referrals

The Collected Best-Practice Referral Wisdom

by

Al Depman, CLU ChFC BH

Practice Management Consultant

Organic Referrals

Table of Contents

Introduction

PART I
Key Organic Referral Concepts

PART II
Organic Referrals and the New Client

Postscript

Introduction

Referrals! We know 'em, we love 'em, we never seem to get enough of 'em.

Every new year many – if not most - of the field producers in the financial services business resolve to "get better at referrals." A worthy resolution, indeed! Of course, the rub is in exactly how you are going to approach this task. The field is littered with poorly implemented, partially executed and half-hearted attempts at referral-gathering.

That's the impetus for this book – creating the holistic concept of Organic Referrals for financial services professionals. I would think that the concept applies in a broader sense to most service and sales professions. But my primary clientele is those of you who market investments, insurance, planning and other financial services to the public.

Organic Referrals has evolved from my work in practice management. All too often, referrals are an after-thought or treated as a separate part of one's practice. Many times the referral procedure is like trying to run a PC program on a Mac computer. The referral system and the producer's business model are incompatible.

Organic Referrals compliment your four geniuses as a financial service professional.
These are:

1. Your ability to initiate new relationships;
2. Your ability to maintain and deepen those relationships;
3. Your ability to inspire people to take action; and
4. Your ability to create the solution and interpret information for the client.

Those geniuses reflect your "art" in our profession. Organic Referrals stem from the art, but reside in the "science" – your business systems. Let's line them up:

Genius/art: initiate new relationships
System/science: Client Acquisition

Genius/art: maintain and deepen relationships
System/science: Client Management

Genius/art: inspiring people to take action
System/science: Sales Process

Genius/art: creating the solution & interpreting information
System/science: Case Development

These are the core four business systems in a practice.

The purpose of approaching referrals from an "organic" perspective is to make sure that they are embedded in each of these systems and complement both your natural geniuses and your business structure design.

The principles in this booklet will serve to do just that.

Up front, let's establish where I, as a practice management consultant, stand on the issue of referrals. The days of the "tacky" referrals are over. A "tacky" referral system is one where you tack on a referral track to the end of each and every interview you have with a prospect or client. It's the way I was brought into the business years ago: as a new rep my sales manager beat the "always ask for referrals" drum, whenever and wherever you saw a prospect or a client. We were given handbooks on how to ask for names and forms for the client to complete (the "I'm not leaving until you give me five names" ultimatum sheet was my favorite). To aid and abet the program, we memorized "objection over-comers" – and were told to handle five objections before giving up – which really wasn't giving up as much as putting the threat off for another day.

It was uncomfortable, confrontational and annoying then and it's even more so now, both to the producer and the client/prospect. In your financial services practice, every business system you implement should be crafted with an eye towards making you "refer-able." This is as the heart of the Organic Referral process: synthesis and continuity rather than tacky bait-and-switch. Good referrals are cultivated and earned. Crummy referrals are a dime a dozen. So, the big question becomes: are you "refer-able?"

Through thousands of practice assessments and producer interviews over the past 28 years I have identified the key leverage points for gathering quality names. These are the best practices in the area of the Client Acquisition system and are consistent with many of the referral processes on the market and supported by firms nationally. The Organic Referral process systematically flows through all of a practice's business systems:

For new clients, it's integrated into the Sales Process and Case Development steps. In particular:
- The Initial interview, where the Iconic Image plays a crucial role and getting permission for introducing the referral concept is established.
- The Discovery Period, which is valuable in getting the client to open up about people who are key members of their fiscal network.

- The Discovery Letter, a hallmark of focused professionalism lending credibility to your refer-ability.
- The Delivery meeting, giving you the first true opportunity to following through on the referral process.

For existing clients Organic Referrals are part of the Client Management System, culminating as part of the annual review meeting agenda.

If the producer has groomed some Centers-of-Influence (COIs), the dedicated name-generation meeting is a best practice for the care and feeding of Organic Referrals.

Organic Referrals might also arise from social & professional networking.

We'll be exploring each of these Organic Referral venues over the course of this booklet.

Terminology

The word "referral" is fraught with all sorts of baggage. As a profession, the financial services business has inherited a negative image over the past century for two things:
- Selling me something "I don't need"

- Badgering me for names of other people to sell them something "they don't need."

Both stem from a highly transactional mindset and a churn'n'burn mentality.

The turnover rate for new producers is abysmal. A company that hires and trains new producers is lucky if they have 20% survive into their fourth year. For many of these terminated souls, they effectively sold product to their friends and family and then left the business, leaving a negative stigma in their wake. Whether the friends and family were sold products they "didn't need" might be debatable, but the summary effect is having additional oft-neglected orphans for the already unwieldy company pool.

On top of that, for most insurance companies, the up-front nature of commissions has discouraged the establishment of a recurring revenue stream business model, forcing the producer to sell ever-increasing amounts of new business to keep their contracts. This exacerbates the transactional nature of how the producer approaches the sales process and, consequently, referrals.

So understandably, many producers avoid the word "referral." They speak of "introductions" instead, or "recommendations." This works. I'll use "referral" since it's a common currency for most of the business world. Feel free to exchange the wording to suit your comfort level.

Also, I use "producer" as a catch-all for advisors, agents, wealth managers, planners, sales associates and any other nomenclature approved and promulgated by various compliance departments. Often I will address you, the producer, directly.

How to use this material

It's important to state up front that you may have a large ship to turn around in the area of referrals. For most of us, the referral process has been less of a process and more of an "app" added to the iPhone of our financial services practice. Organic Referrals are embedded in the basic programming of your iPhone (if you will allow me the metaphor!).

When I ask experienced producers where the majority of their top-tier clients have come from, the number one source across the various platforms is "referrals." In customer satisfaction surveys conducted by producers I've worked with over the years, most top-tier clients claim to be willing to refer their particular producer to others. When pursued on this claim, many actually do so...*when asked*!

What follows is a comprehensive set of pieces collectively known as the Organic Referral process. It's designed to be implemented piece by piece, gradually over time, in any order that makes sense in your practice.

One lesson I've learned over my years of consulting with producers is the simple truth that nothing really gets done and truly implemented unless there is an accountability partner. The accountability partner can be a peer producer, a strong assistant, field manager, mentor, spouse or an outside person willing to take on the role of helping you be the best professional you can be.

The accountability person is someone to role-play these concepts with, to give them some reality testing and to hold you to the day-to-day integration into your mindset and actions.

With all this in mind, let's go about the work of sowing some Organic Referral seeds for harvesting over the rest of your career!

Part I
Key Organic Referral Concepts

Chapter 1
The Big Four Referral Questions
or
Am I Even Refer-able?

The situation is a common one. Bill, the producer, is summing up at the end of a meeting with Carl, a client. Perhaps it's an annual review, a closing appointment, a plan presentation, or a service call. There is a sense of completion, and Carl is ready to move on to other things in his day.

There is an uncomfortable pause. Bill isn't quite finished.

"Carl, before I go, I wanted to ask if you've been satisfied with the products and services we've been discussing and implementing."

"Certainly, Bill," he says, shifting uncomfortably in his chair.

"That's great. As you know, my main source of new clients is through the referral process. Nothing beats a personal recommendation," Bill smiles.

"I see," Carl says, thinking how to end this quickly.

"Who do you know who might benefit from my services?" Bill's question is more like a statement.

Carl seems to ponder this, looking up at the ceiling. Bill is patient in his silence.

Carl finally speaks. "No one comes to mind right now, but I'll keep you in mind. Do you have any business cards I can hand out?"

Ball back in his court, Bill fumbles in his pocket.

"Certainly. Here are a few. I appreciate your help." Carl accepts the cards and puts them into his jacket pocket. Bill rises and they shake hands. Both men depart, feeling relieved.

Another "asking for referrals" event is over.

What's wrong with this picture?

Primarily, of course, no names were gathered. Maybe Bill left the appointment feeling that he had set the stage for future referrals. Carl felt he had dodged a bullet; after carrying around the business cards for a few days, he would stash them into a drawer that seldom gets opened.

The reality is that the referral process goes far deeper than this brief encounter. What we just witnessed—the actual asking for the names—is just the tip of the referral iceberg. My best-practices research suggests that there are considerations that need to be addressed prior to a true referral experience. These findings are summarized in the producer's ability to answer four key questions:

1. **Is there any chance this client will give me a referral?**
2. **What is the client thinking when I broach the topic of referrals?**
3. **Am I even "refer-able?"**
4. **What value do I bring that is sufficiently unique to warrant an introduction?**

Let's dig in to these questions.

1. The history question: Is there any chance this client will give me a referral?

Bill needs to determine Carl's referral history. Has he had negative, neutral, or positive experiences? Perhaps Carl has been burned by the process in the past and will never provide a referral again. Knowing this would save everyone a lot of time. Carl would then need to be brought around gradually, over a long period of time, if ever. On the other hand, if Carl has had neutral or positive experiences with referrals, the outlook is brighter.

A simple question can be asked at an appropriate time during a meeting with Carl.

"Carl, my primary marketing tool is word-of-mouth introductions. This means I rely on good clients like you to spread the word and promote me and what I do. If you don't mind, could you tell me about your past experience in referring professionals to people that you know personally and through work?"

Allow the client to vent, if necessary. Giving them an opportunity to speak about referrals – positive, negative or neutral - is a powerful step towards actually getting names. A strong finish to this conversation might be:

"What would it take for me to earn a good referral from you, Carl?"

2. The psychology question: What's the client thinking when I broach the topic of referrals?

Primarily, the client is weighing the impact you will have on their relationships. Most people have three levels of relationships. The **A** level relationships are the most intimate and critical to the client, personally and/or professionally. **B** level relationships are important, but not as intimate. **C** level relationships are more like acquaintances.

As Carl is looking at Bill, he is subconsciously deciding if it's worth risking relationships to introduce him to people he knows. Bill can have one of three levels of impact on a relationship. He can enhance it, have a neutral effect, or disrupt it.

An ENHANCED relationship is one in which the referred person thanks Carl for introducing Bill into his or her life.

A NEUTRAL effect has the referral understanding why Carl provided the introduction, but is not interested. Bill is gently rebuffed; no harm done.

A DISRUPTED relationship is one where the referral calls Carl up the next day and demands to know, "Why did you unleash an insurance agent on me?"

If Carl is not confident in how Bill will treat the relationship, there is no way he will provide an A or B level person as a referral. Perhaps he will offer a C level person to Bill since he's not too concerned about ruining that relationship; if Bill happens to make that C relationship stronger, all the better.

Carl would be much more likely to refer an A or a B prospect if he was sure Bill's contact would result in a call thanking him for the introduction.

The relationship issue is a primary concern for Carl. Word-of-mouth is so much simpler when the stakes are not so high. Carl would have little trouble referring Bill if Bill was offering a hot product sure to save a friend some money or had an inside scoop on some new high tech gadget. The more transactional the perceived value of Bill's offering, the easier the referral. Many advisors allow themselves to slip into this transactional mode when asking for referrals.

Newer advisors will often use language similar to this: "I know I can save the people you know some money with the products we offer. Who can you think of that would like to look into saving some money?" Or, "Our portfolio analysts are the best. Do you know anyone who would appreciate a fresh look at comparing investment managers?"

These tracks pull the referral process into the transaction realm. The net result is that the advisor falls into the stereotypical higher-pressure referral-jockey trap of the old insurance days.

Those days are gone. Your client may still have this old-school baggage about referrals. The WORST thing you can do is pander to it, ensuring a future of nothing but C quality name-gathering.

In short, you need to direct your client's mindset from product/transaction to you and your relationship. Are you up to it? That's what Organic Referrals are all about.

The primary concept to keep in mind when answering these first two questions is that you are asking to be brought into an existing relationship that your client has with a friend, relative, or business associate.

Your client is consciously and subconsciously evaluating the potential impact you will have on that relationship. In addition, you should explore your client's experience with referrals in order to understand why he or she might be reluctant to provide you with names.

Both of the above questions uncover your client's biases. These are pre-existing conditions in the referral process and are not likely to change until you have had a chance to prove yourself as a trustworthy, mindful, and courteous handler of referrals.

Now we consider the second two questions of our original four that can have an immediate impact on you and your business:

Am I referable?

What value do I bring that is sufficiently unique to warrant an introduction?

3. The reality question: Am I even referable?

Much of the work around this question has already been done, for better or worse. When you sit down with a top client or center-of-influence and prepare to ask for introductions, the experiences you both have shared have a direct impact on the referral discussion. Your client, understandably, will project his or her own history with you on any name he or she might divulge.

Based on my interviews with advisors, external factors are important to consider. For example, did you consistently respect your client's time? An advisor who keeps his cell phone on or checks text messages constantly while in a meeting with a client shows little respect for that client's time. Your client will remember that, and assume you will treat any referrals the same way. What are the chances of obtaining a referral in that case? Slim to none.

How do you present yourself? Your image is another critical factor in being refer-able. How you dress, the jewelry you wear, grooming, makeup, manners, and sense of humor all have a bearing on a client's decision to introduce you to someone.

If you are serious about referrals, there are three steps you can take to get an objective sense of your professional image:

- Look at yourself in a full-length mirror with a mentor or trusted associate. Ask them to be frank about what they see.
- Have another advisor work with you by observing you during discovery and presentation meetings and then provide feedback immediately after the meetings.
- Videotape yourself in a simulated referral appointment. Again, have a trusted associate or mentor provide feedback.

Being refer-able also hinges on the *perceived value* you bring to your client relationship. Thus:

4. The reason question: What value do I bring that is sufficiently unique to warrant an introduction?

The following instance is taken from my case files:

Tricia is a sharp, confident advisor. She feels good about her image and her practice. She's meeting with April Burgess, a top client. April owns an architecture firm in Menlo Park and has been a client of Tricia's for more than five years. They meet formally once a year for a full review; it is during this meeting that Tricia asks for introductions.

April has provided Tricia with a few referrals over the years, but Tricia knows they are not her top-shelf relationships. Today, April suggested Tricia call two building contractors she works with. These are medium-tier referrals that will result in medium-level clients. Tricia would like to be referred upward to April's peers in the architecture world:

"April, I appreciate the names. As usual, I will let you know what happens with them. But I did have someone else I'd like to ask about."

"Sure, Trish, who is it?"

"A.J. Ostenberg. The owner of O&S Realty. He's the kind of businessperson I've been targeting this year and think he'd be a great addition to my practice."

April thought for a moment. "I do know A.J. through our community work with the Make-A-Wish Foundation." She paused. "But I know he's got someone he works with. So I don't think it would work."

Tricia backed off, not wanting to seem pushy.

What happened here? Everything was going well, but Tricia couldn't get the upward-referral. Why not?

The tell-tale sentence uttered by April is the core issue: "I know he's got someone he works with." What she is actually saying is: "He's got somebody he's working with who I assume is doing the same job for him as you are doing for me."

April sees all advisors as bringing the same value to their clients. In her mind, all advisors are the same. Tricia hasn't brought anything unique to the table, at least as far as April can see. Tricia hasn't provided a compelling reason to be introduced to A.J. Ostenberg.

Having worked with Tricia, I know she brings a unique perspective to her financial planning. She has a CPA background and has developed a great presentation on the tax climate that looks back 30 years and forward 30 years. This is a very effective tool in providing a perspective for those about to retire. In the context of the presentation, she introduces various products that provide possible tax-free, tax-deferred, and taxable income streams.

We worked on helping Tricia see that her tax perspective is a fresh view on traditional retirement planning. She not only needed to realize her presentation was unique but also needed to refine the language to articulate it. Tricia must be able to demonstrate to April that an introduction to A.J. would be a good thing, whether or not he chooses to take advantage of it.

We played it out all the way: if April gives an introduction to A.J., what should April say? Here's what we came up with:

"A.J., you'll be getting a call from Tricia Carpenter. She's my advisor and has a really good perspective on tax planning for retirement that I thought you would appreciate. I think it would be worth 15 minutes to check it out. She'll even buy the cup of coffee."

If A.J. balks and says, "Thanks, but I already have a person I work with," April needs to be confident enough recommending Tricia to reply, "I thought you might. What Tricia brings to the table is a great complement to what you are already doing. I know you're always looking for new perspectives. A.J., I think it would be worth a few minutes."

Tricia couldn't ask for much more!

Question for you: what is your unique perspective that warrants the client or center-of-influence to go that extra step and REALLY recommend you after the initial knee-jerk reaction?

It's a combination of art and science and comes into view as the "Iconic Image."

Chapter 2
Your Value Proposition: The Iconic Image

A common sight in downtown locations during the holidays is the Salvation Army or United Way mega-thermometer. This visual device indicates the progress being made in reaching the contribution goal. As the red "dollar-mercury" rises to the 100%-of-goal point, the pedestrians, shoppers, and commuters are getting a sense of fulfillment and anticipation of a successful donation drive.

A number of producers I work with employ a similar visual image in their practices. They report many advantages to implementing this "iconic image." Mike's experience provides us with an excellent case study.

Mike is an experienced advisor in Minnesota who recently retired and sold his practice to Brad. One of the hallmarks of his practice was – and is, since Brad has picked it up and continues to run with it – the simple financial pyramid. You've seen a variation of this plenty of times: a standard-issue pyramid that has five (+/-) layers:

- The base is all about the basics: budget & debt management, 3-6 month reserve emergency fund, and a risk management program.

- Layer 2: Safety & Liquidity: Mortgage, bank and fixed products.
- Layer 3: Capital Accumulation. Included here are real estate (home, rental), mutual funds, securities, cash values of insurance, annuities, and other savings.
- Layer 4: Tax-advantaged Investments. Qualified money, Roth IRAs, matching funds.
- Layer 5: Estate and Legacy Planning.

Mike told me about his strategy in using it.

"The first time the client sees it is in the initial meeting," he says. "I use it to set the stage for our work together. I used to just talk about how I help people with their financial planning. Then I was reading that people only remember 20% of what they hear. Turns out they remember 50% of what they *see* and hear…and 90% of what they see, hear and *interact with*. The light bulb went on. So I adopted the pyramid as the visual element."

"Can you tell me more about the interactive part?" I asked.

"On the initial meeting, I slide the pyramid across the desk as I talk through it. After I'm done I ask a simple question: 'So where do you feel you are in this pyramid?' and shut up. Invariably, they point to a layer or touch the page. At that point, I know they've bought into the concept – interacted with it – and are giving me an entry point."

"So it acts like an icon on a computer desktop. Click it and it opens up a program. The client touches the pyramid and opens up the sales process," I summarized.

"Exactly," Mike agreed. "But the power of the image comes much later. I continue with the planning process and build the solution for the client. When we get agreement on the solutions and begin implementing them I bring the pyramid back out. The dialogue goes something like this…"

Mike pulls out his laminated copy of the pyramid and addresses me as he would the client.

"Remember when we reviewed this pyramid back in our initial meeting? Let's look at it again in light of the work we've done together. When we began (he points to a spot on the second layer) you were here. Now, we are here (pointing to level three). Progress! We're building your financial success."

"You said 'you were here, now we are here,'" I noticed. "A deliberate choice of words?"

"Caught that, aye?" Mike smiled. "Yep, they could only get so far on their own, but together we make progress."

"What does this all accomplish?"

"We establish growth and change visually, and reinforce the pyramid image. In addition, while there is satisfaction in filling in the pyramid, it shows the opportunity still remaining. Today level three, tomorrow level four. The groundwork for future growth – and business – has been laid."

"Is that the last they see of the pyramid?" I asked.

Mike laughed. "Not by a long shot. It's a recurring image every year at the annual review. Over and over I use it as a barometer of growth towards their ultimate financial security and success. The wonderful side effect is that it's very refer-able. I get calls from folks my client have talked to who say 'Mike, Ed said I should see this pyramid you use.' We have some fun with the 'pyramid scheme' phrase, but the recommendation puts any negative connotations to rest."

Mike uses the iconic image of the pyramid to deliver his value proposition and then to mark progress over time. In my work with advisors over the years I've seen any number of iconic images successfully implemented: circles, roadmaps, lines, boxes, periodic charts, sailboats, puzzles, financial houses, buckets, trees, baseball diamonds, spigots...all tailored to the style and personality of the advisor. They all have Mike's three dimensions of adult learning:

- Verbal
- Visual
- Interactive

One final thought on the use of the iconic image from Mike.

"The most important use is in my practice transition. Because of the pyramid, as I was introducing Brad to my clients as he was taking over, the clients could articulate to Brad where they were in context of the pyramid. They'd say things like 'Mike got me up here to level 3. I expect you to get me to level 4.' Or 'Mike got my pyramid up to the top. Can you do the same for my kids?' Brad was amazed and all he needs to do is continue using the established image. It certainly made the transition much, much smoother."

OK. Add "awesome transition tool" to the reasons why an iconic image is a best practice. I can provide a copy of the pyramid Mike (and now Brad) uses. Just send a request to practicedoc@gmail.com.

Chapter 3
The Five Best Practice Elements of the Organic Referral Process

When all is said and done on the topic of referrals, there emerge five best practice elements that seem to permeate most of the successful systems producers use. So naturally we will adopt these as the fundamental tenets of the Organic Referral process. Each of these best practices ultimately needs to be in place for the acquisition of quality prospects. They are:

1. **No surprises!**
2. **Ensure your client knows what you do and how to promote you.**
3. **Ensure your client knows you seek relationships not just transactions.**
4. **Help your client focus on the referrals you want.**
5. **Obtain a personal introduction...and follow through.**

Let's take a close look at each one.

1. No surprises!

The best referral processes I've encountered are open, honest and freely discussed. This is a hallmark of the Organic Referral method. Discomfort in asking for referrals leads to many awkward moments and often come across as bait-and-switch operations. The classic "bait" is the initial reason you are seeing the client – a review, service work, sales appointment – and the "switch" occurs when you're finished with the stated agenda and shift gears to asking for referrals. No warning, just the uncomfortable "now before I leave..." tacked on segue. Tacky, indeed.

If you are planning to ask for referrals when meeting with a client, get permission prior to the event. When setting up the appointment or in the appointment's confirmation, simply add:

"...and after we're finished with the paperwork, Jan, would it be alright if we discussed a couple of introductions I have in mind?" or:
"...would you mind if we spend a couple of minutes brainstorming names of possible prospects?" or:
"...would it be okay if I ran some word-of-mouth marketing ideas past you?"

This "no surprises" concept forces you, the producer, to be prepared for the referral encounter, ensuring that it's not a quick "who do ya know..." slapped on the end of a meeting, Rather, it should be a more professional experience.

Frank, a producer I've worked with in Tennessee, is now getting a regular flow of referrals from his clientele.

"I don't even ask," he tells me. "I just let them all know all the time. Asking for referrals is a non-event since I consistently remind them of my availability to those they know and love. Don't keep me a secret. When they see me or get a call from me or Cathy, my assistant, the referral idea has been so well planted that they respond with names."

Frank, Cathy and I are working on the next level of name-generation to refine the quality of the names even further. Frank's referral process is Organic – that is, it permeates all of his business systems. Frank, Cathy and the clients are all constantly (organically, systemically) keen to the referral issue.

2. Ensure your client (or center-of-influence) knows what you do and how to promote you to others.

Your client should have an awareness of the depth and breadth of your products and services so he or she can effectively articulate the value you can provide to a prospect. The best practice in this self-introduction is to have an iconic image presentation: one with memorable verbal, visual and interactive elements.

Chapter Two covered the iconic image and its use as a tool. With a visual icon to work with, your value proposition can more easily be transferred to your referral source. The idea is to embrace an icon that best represents your practice. It should reflect your products and services, your process in working with a client and your passion for the business.

3. Ensure your client knows that you seek relationships, not just transactions.

This is much more difficult than it might sound. Through most of the last century in our business "referrals" meant finding someone to sell something to. You can expect this mentality to be embedded quite deeply in most people and your ability to dispel this mentality is paramount. The client or center-of-influence might like you, appreciate your process and passion but still hold back on quality names because he still feels he's "siccing an insurance guy" on them.

You need to establish your credibility so a client won't feel that by introducing you to a prospect, his or her relationship with that prospect will be harmed. We discussed this in Chapter One. Developing language to suggest the desire to find a longer-term relationship and not a hit-and-run quick sale is critical. For example:

"What I would like to do is identify good quality people in your network of acquaintances. With your permission, I'd like to contact these folks and meet with them for 15 minutes or so. During that time, I'll review what I do, sharing that iconic (house/pyramid/circle) image, and find out if they have any questions I might be able to answer. At that point, with their permission, I'll stay in touch with them. Down the road, when the time comes for them to make a financial decision, I hope to be the one they turn to. Does that sound like a fair way of doing business?"

Note the last sentence. The producer asks if this is a fair way of doing business. You need to have this permission to move forward (see Organic Referral best practice #1 above). At this point, 25% of the clients will still avoid giving referrals. They won't ever do so, no matter how persuasive you might be. For cultural, genetic, psychological or religious reasons, referrals are taboo to these folks. Accept that and move on.

However, for the other 75% of the population, there's the potential for names. These people fall into two categories: limited and unlimited.

Limited referrers are those who have a finite number of possible referrals – their influence just doesn't go very far or is not with your target client profile. You need to determine this as soon as possible, for once you've gotten all the limited number of names available, it will be counter-productive to continue asking. They're done – tapped out, finished.

Unlimited referrers are people who have a deep well of contacts that is being constantly refreshed. Examples of unlimited referrers include professionals who have large client bases and are in regular contact with them; human resource directors who are involved with the ebb and flow of personnel at medium-to-large organizations; training and development leaders who have quality individuals cycling through their courses; and anyone in a community who has active networks socially and/or personally.

Whether the referrer is limited or unlimited, be sure that they know you are looking to leverage their influence to form new relationships. More importantly, these new relationships will need to reflect well on the referrer.

4. Help the client focus on the referrals you want: The market focus list.

Whenever I stay in a Marriott property, I usually receive an e-mail a week later asking me to complete a short survey on my experience. Being a good patron and always happy to provide feedback,

I agree and click onto the site. Most of the survey is rating specific items one-through-ten. How was the pillow? Was the staff friendly? Was your rug clean? No problem...I click away.

Then I get to the last part of the survey, a big blank box with the instruction: "Please tell us anything else you would like about your stay." Uh-oh. Up until now, I was reacting merrily to the questions. Now the survey is asking me to actually think. Since that's too much effort, I usually end it there and hit the "submit" button. Woe to the survey that forces me to put words into the big blank box before allowing me to submit it! In that case, I move from compliance to frustration.

Bottom line: I prefer to react to one-through-ten button pushing rather than proactively filling in the big blank box. In school I also preferred true/false and multiple choice tests to essays or fill-in-the-blanks. It's human nature to prefer to react – it's quicker and requires less effort than forcing us to think too much. (I'll let the philosophers worry about what this means for the future of humanity – it works here for our purposes!)

So it is with the Organic Referral process. To help gather good quality names, the producer needs to help the client focus on the types of names, situations or demographics being sought. Giving the referrer something to react to prevents his mind from going global, in which case he tends to be overwhelmed and simply shuts down and says: "give me some business cards and let me think about it."

This help in focusing requires the producer to have done some homework to prepare for the referral encounter.

An exercise that aids in focusing the client or center-of-influence on specific people is the Mapping Exercise. The producer sets aside a few minutes prior to meeting with the client and mentally (or on paper) runs through the following list of possible names that might be appropriate to present as "prompts" in the referral discussion.

What contacts could the client possibly have when you think about their:

- Family
- Relatives
- Friends
- Professionals (close working relationships)
- Business organizational structure
- Community involvement
- Worship
- Non-profit/volunteer activities
- Sports activities
- Hobbies

- Networks this person has access to personally and professionally
- Key people that this person might communicate with personally and professionally

This exercise culminates in the formation of a "Market Focus List." This Market Focus List consists of a listing of the types of people you are interested in meeting. The more specific, the better.

Joe, an advisor in Minneapolis, has a Market Focus List that includes the names of three executives at a large Twin Cities firm that he would like to have as clients. Joe tells me:
"Everyone I meet who might know someone who could introduce me to these execs, I ask for the contact information. I know that these three executives will make my year and I can really, really help them maximize their benefit packages."

This is a technique for upgrading Joe's referral profile. Find the people you would like to make clients and pursue them from multiple angles.

A Market Focus List may simply contain a bulleted list of the types of people you are interested in meeting...and why. The following is a sample of a market focus list from Gerry, an advisor in northern Iowa:

- Architects
- Business Owners
- Small Businesses (under 50 employees)
- Ages 60 - 85 (post-retirement)
- Farm Families
- Church-involved
- Ag-related Business
- Interstates Electric
- Construction Management
- Community Involved
- Accounting

Presenting the referrer with this list should be followed by a reason you are interested in that market and an example of how you've helped someone.

For architects, Gerry's language is:

"Architects are interesting to work with. I interned in an architecture firm for a couple of summers in college and found their ability to take a concept, design a plan and build an actual structure from those plans to be fascinating. I've gone back to that firm and learned about their benefits package and was able to offer some enhancements, so I'm getting to know that market pretty well. Who do you know that is a good quality person involved in the architectural world?"

If appropriate, Gerry provides specific names to the client. To continue the architect track, when he is with an architect client, Gerry will present a list of architecture firms in the area pulled from the internet. At that point, he'll ask if the client might provide some insight or contact information for anyone on the list. This would warm up an otherwise cold approach:

"I'm considering contacting all of these firms for a benefits review. Who on this list are you familiar with? Can you introduce me to anyone in these firms?"

Some producers use the Market Focus List as a laminated piece they keep in their presentation materials. Others keep it more informal, recalling the list from memory and writing names on a yellow pad.

Gerry offers this advice: "Use a few bullet points each time you have a referral meeting – don't overwhelm the client! Allow them to learn who and what you are looking for over time. The best referrals will come after the client is satisfied that the process is smooth and non-invasive."

Formal or informal, the best practice is to help the referrer focus as much as possible so that they have every chance to help you.

5. Obtain a personal introduction...and follow through.

The best referrals, naturally, are when the referrer introduces the producer to the prospect. Everything we've discussed in the Organic Referral process up to now culminates in the personal introduction. To summarize the booklet to this point:

Examine your answers to the questions posed in Chapter One:
> History: Based on his or her experience in the past, is there any chance this client will give me a referral?
> Psychology: What is the client thinking when I broach the topic of referrals?
> Reality: Am I even referable?

> Reason: What value do I bring that is sufficiently unique to warrant a referral?

Do you have an Iconic Image (Chapter Two)? If so, how are you utilizing it to reinforce your value proposition verbally, visually and interactively?

The careful implementation of the first four Organic Referral best practice steps thus far in Chapter Three:
> No surprises!
> Ensuring your client knows what you do and how to promote you.
> Ensuring your client knows you are looking for relationships, not just transactions.
> Help the client focus on the referrals you want via a Market Focus List.

Once all of these issues have been adequately addressed we can ask for the introductions. There are a number of ways the referrer can provide an introduction for you. He or she might:
- Make an outreach call or email to the referral preparing her for your initial call
- Write a note of introduction on your brochure or other promotional piece
- Agree to personally introduce you to the referral at an upcoming event

John, an advisor in Pittsburgh, tells me that his preference is to not leave it up to the referrer to do the introduction. Instead, he asks:

"I'll be giving Jules a call (or sending Jules an email) later this week. If it's okay with you, I'll mention your name. If you'd like to let Jules know I'll be contacting her, all the better. Is that fair?"

As we saw earlier, if the client hesitates or seems unsure, the reassuring verbiage is:

"With your permission, Bill, I'd like to contact Jules and meet with her for 15 minutes or so. During that time, I'll review what I do, sharing that iconic (house/pyramid/circle) image, and find out if she has any questions I might be able to answer. At that point, with her permission, I'll stay in touch with Jules. Down the road, when the time comes for her to make a financial decision, I hope to be the one she turns to. Does that sound like a fair way of doing business?"

With the new referral in hand, the ball is now in the producer's court. How you handle the subsequent communications and meetings with the referral will determine how open clients and centers-of-influence will be in the future. Some best practices around this follow-through:

- Keep the referrer in the loop as you contact the referral. Since you are impacting two relationships, be sure that the referrer hears from both you and the referral.
- A note of appreciation for the referral would be appropriate.
- Perhaps invite the referrer to lunch or to an event to show your gratitude.
- *Never* offer cash or gifts for referrals. Organic Referrals are relationship-based, not transactional.

Part II
Organic Referrals
and the New Client:
Integration into the Sales Process

Chapter 4
The Initial Interview

In the world of the Organic Referral process, it's never too early to promote the concept of building your practice by word-of-mouth introductions.

With a new client (or, more precisely, client-to-be a.k.a. prospect), the initial interview is a pivotal first encounter. In it, you:

- create a dialogue with the prospect
- get to know their specific situation
- communicate your value proposition
- get agreement to work together, and
- discuss compensation.

It's during the last step that the referral topic is broached. The producer should be looking to be as transparent as possible when it comes to compensation. Every week I see postings and articles in the media warning consumers to beware how producers are paid. So it behooves you to get the issue on the table in the first meeting.

The classic phrase many of us learned early on in our careers was:

"I'm paid in three ways. If it's a plan or investments, there is a fee involved. If it's insurance products, the companies pay me a commission. The third way I'm compensated is through referrals. If you find the work we do together is valuable, I simply ask for introductions to others who might also find it valuable. Is that fair?"

That's it. No asking for names at that point. Simply open up the door to referrals and get agreement that after the work is done, it's fair game to discuss them. If the person you are talking to is a referral, don't hesitate to remind them of that. It's now an expectation.

Congratulations – you've begun to produce Organic Referrals!

Chapter 5
The Discovery Period

The second step in the sales process is the Discovery Period.

The discovery period is defined as those interactions – meetings, calls, emails - when you are eliciting information from the client. If all you are doing is gathering enough information to sell a product, you are engaged in what I call a **TRANSACTIONAL** discovery process.

However, if you are reading this booklet, my suspicion is that you prefer a **RELATIONSHIP** discovery process. This means you are also asking about their feelings and probing for the client's perspective on what financial health means to them. And names. A hallmark of the Organic Referral process is the ability to coax out names of key players in the client's fiscal life.

When Mike, our financial advisor, took my wife and me through his discovery process, we participated in a truly relational, Organic Referral experience.

He did the fact-finding, using his standard discovery booklet and when prompted, asked about our will:

"Who's the executor?" Mike asked.

"My wife's sister, Carla," I replied.

"She'll be the one who gets the kids if you both die in a common accident?"

"Yes."

Mike looked up. "Tell me about why you chose Carla."

"Well, she lives close by, has kids about the same age, she's smart and her values are solid," I said.

"Great!" Mike exclaimed and made some notes in his booklet.

Mike then went on to our $750,000 worth of life insurance policies:

"Let's see. You are each other's beneficiaries. Secondary beneficiaries are the children. Again, in a common accidental death, who is the guardian for the children since they are all under 18?"

"My mom is, I think" I answered, trying to remember.

"Tell me about Mom," Mike stated.

"She's 85, lives in Arizona, still feisty and independent."

Mike nodded and again made notes. Before leaving the topic, he said:

"One more item. As we were talking over the executor and guardian roles, are either of you in those roles for someone else?"

I'd never been asked that before. "Actually, my uncle appointed me executor of his will ten years ago. He's 77 now, lives in Philly, and I had forgotten about that."

"Tell me about your uncle," Mike probed.

"He's a widower, no children, lives alone in a condo and is getting frail."

Again, Mike took notes.

At the conclusion of the meeting, Mike turned to us:

"There could be a problem here. In the improbable event of you both dying simultaneously, Carla gets to raise the kids and Mom gets the money on their behalf. Is that how you'd like it to go?"

My wife and I looked at each other.

"Well, no," my wife said. "Carla and my mother-in-law, Betty, have never met. Carla is 30 and Betty is almost 86."

"That would be an awkward situation," I agreed.

"Would it be wise to have Carla as executor *and* guardian of the life insurance proceeds?" Mike suggested.

"Yes!" we responded in unison. Paperwork ensued.

Mike proceeded to assemble our financial plan. We received a letter from him in the interim (an awesome, polished step - see the next chapter: The Discovery Letter) and when he was ready to set up the implantation meeting his assistant Laura called.

"Hi, Al, this is Laura from Mike's office. He'd like to schedule a meeting to review your financial plan and implementation of specific action items."

"Of course, Laura," I replied and we set the date and time.

"And one last thing, Al," Laura added. "Mike would like to ask if it's okay after the formal part of the meeting is over if he could spend a few minutes discussing his word-of-mouth marketing."

"As in referrals?" I laughed. "Fine with us."

"Exactly," Laura stated. "See you then."

The genius of what Mike was doing was pure Organic Referral philosophy. He was coaxing us to discuss names of people in our fiscal network. We opened up about Carla, Mom and my uncle. The consequence was that these three people are now "on the table" and eligible for feeding back. We were being disarmed by Mike. The results would soon be evident.

We held the plan review and implementation in Mike's office. At the end of the meeting, he said:

"I appreciate all your business. As I suggested at our initial meeting, one of the key ways I'm compensated is that if you found this process valuable, we might be able to discuss introductions to others that might also find this valuable. Is that fair?"

"Fair enough," I answered.

Mike picked up his yellow pad on which some names were scrawled.
"I was reviewing my notes and would you mind if I gave Carla a call?"

"I suppose," I said. He knew about Carla from the discovery meeting when we had divulged her name.

"But why?" my wife interjected. This was her sister, after all.

Mike sat back. "You described her as a bright lady. Tell me, has she ever been the executor of a will before?"

"No, she hasn't," my wife replied.

"Has she ever been in receipt of $750,000 in death benefits on someone else's behalf?"

"Again, no."

"What I'd like to do, with your permission, is contact Carla. My purpose will be to hopefully meet with her and review a booklet she can keep that describes what the duties of an executor are, what documents are needed, samples of letters that need to be filed and a whole host of resources she can turn to."

Mike reached into his desk drawer and pulled out the booklet (<u>What Do You Do Now?</u> From LIMRA) and slid it across the desk.

"In addition, I'd like to discuss the wishes you two have for how that $750,000 death benefit is to be used for the health and education of your children. Would you mind if I gave Carla call?"

We were stunned. In all our years of dealing with insurance and investment people, Mike was the first one to go that one step farther. We had an overwhelming sense of peace, knowing that he'd be there to oversee the process if the worst were to happen and knowing that Carla would be prepped for her role.

"Yes," we agreed. "Please do."

"Thank you," Mike responded. "And Al, you are the executor of your uncle's estate. Do you have a guide for that role?"

"Uh, no. I'm petty clueless about it, actually."

Mike pushed the booklet to me. "This one's yours. I suggest you review it with your uncle before it's too late."

He did call Carla, met with her and her husband, and they became clients as well. Mike is very referable thanks to his practical, value-added systems and we've sent others his way.

So how deep is your discovery process? Does it –
your fact-finder - prompt you to ask for the
following names?

- Executor of the will (or, if no will, who
  would likely be in that role)
- Beneficiaries (primary, secondary and
  tertiary)–and why they were chosen -does it
  line up logically with the other roles, such as
  executor or trustee?
- Trustee
- Guardian
- Powers-of-attorney
- Benefits person at work
- Attorney
- CPA
- P&C agent
- Who they've turned to for financial advice in
  the past
- Business associates with a financial interest in
  your client
- Other people who might have a specific role
  in your client's fiscal life

If the client asks what you need the name for, some
sample response language might be as follows:

"In my role as your financial advisor (planner, agent, quarterback, coach, etc.), I am ready and able to coordinate all the various people who impact your financial health. Does that make sense? What I'd like to do at this point is to simply identify and note those important people."

"Once we've established your financial game plan, we may need to contact some or all of them to ensure they know their role in how you'd like your plan to proceed and play out. That's part of our service, trying not to leave anything to chance. Would you agree?"

One final note on this discovery process: You are well served by gathering these names and feeding them back in later interviews (as Mike did). Be sure to ask the client if he or she is engaged in those same roles for others (as Mike demonstrated). Are they executors? Guardians? Beneficiaries? Your client may need the same advice that I did in my role as executor for my uncle. These may be future opportunities for acquiring assets, and growing your business. Even if they aren't, you are certainly deepening the relationships with your top-tier clients.

Chapter 6
The Discovery Letter

The discovery letter is a document that summarizes where things stand. It's designed to arrive midway between the discovery period and the presentation meeting. The timing is designed to keep you top-of-mind with the prospective client. If there is no communication between discovery and presentation, the producer often drops off the prospect's radar screen. When this happens, the producer needs to spend a good deal of time reconstructing the reasons for what will be presented and recommended.

The discovery letter provides a "heads-up" that you're diligently working on their behalf and will be seeing them soon. In providing your client value, as the discovery letter does, you immediately become more refer-able in the Organic Referral process.

The elements of a best-practices Discovery Letter are:

"I appreciate your time"
"Here's what I heard you say"
"These are your priorities as I recorded them"
"I'm working to use your available resources to address those priorities"
"If any of this is incorrect, please call"
"Here's when we'll be meeting again"

There are many reasons why the discovery letter is a best practice:

- It keeps the prospect involved while the case is being prepared
- It's a professional touch
- It gives the client a respectful opportunity to change their mind
- It's a great piece to have in the file for compliance purposes
- It can provide the agenda for the presentation meeting by addressing those priorities in sequence
- It can be used to quickly get a third-party up to speed. This third-party is someone who shows up at the presentation but didn't attend any of the other meetings

Here's a sample discovery letter.

Dear Prospect/Client,

We at (practice name) would like to take this opportunity to thank you for engaging us for your financial needs. We would like to assure you that we will continue to make every effort to fulfill your needs and exceed your expectations. It is our desire to provide you with a tailored experience that will leave you confident that you have made a wise decision to work with [insert practice name].

During our meeting last (day, date), we covered a substantial amount of information. While it may have seemed overwhelming at times, we believe it is crucial to take the time to gain a full and complete understanding of your needs, wants and desires. To this end, below I have itemized your most important goals as I understand them:

1. *Assure a comfortable retirement for Mary and Bill.*
2. *Minimize taxation during retirement*
3. *Minimize expenses and taxes during the transfer of your assets to your heirs, Sarah, Emily, and Bill Jr.*
4. *Create a family foundation to support the University of Notre Dame, the American Red Cross, and the Center for the Arts.*

If you have any additional concerns, or if you have reconsidered your priorities after further discussion and thought, please feel free to contact me. As we discussed, we will prepare a presentation for your review at our meeting next [insert day] at [insert time], using the resources we identified.

Again, thank you for choosing [insert practice name].
Sincerely,

Chapter 7
The Delivery:
Organic Referrals Come Full Cycle in the
Sales Process

The delivery meeting is the time when you mark the official transition of a prospect becoming a client. This face-to-face event with your new client:

- reinforces the purpose of the plan you've developed for them,
- establishes what you've done together in the context of the Iconic Image,
- plants the seeds for the next opportunity, and
- covers the service expectations you and your team will provide on an ongoing basis.

This is also the first time when you have formally earned the right to ask for referrals. Why? The planning/product solution process is complete and your client can look back and see the value you have brought to his or her life. We saw last chapter that as part of the discovery process, you can collect and record names of people important to your client's financial life. Now is the time to start asking for introductions (as Mike did).

It might sound like this:

"I appreciate your confidence in my (our) process. You may recall that earlier we discussed the fact that we have a great many resources at our disposal to help you and those who are important to the execution of this plan we've put in place.

"I'd like to reach out to some of those people to ensure that they are aware of their role in your plan and to see if they require - or would like - additional information on how best to carry out that role to your specifications.

"You named Jane doe as the executor of your will. Would you mind if I contact Jane? My purpose would be to provide her with a booklet on what an executor can expect and what resources to turn to in the unlikely event of a simultaneous death."

Similar phrasing can be used for trustees, beneficiaries, guardians, powers-of-attorney, and anyone else you may wish to contact. There are documents and checklists for each of these roles that can be obtained from a number of sources including attorneys you are seeking to develop reciprocal relationships with.

Note that in setting up the delivery meeting, it's important to adhere to the "no surprises" best practice and ask permission to bring up the topic of referrals. It's polite, courteous and bespeaks professionalism.

Part III
Organic Referrals and the Existing Client

Chapter 8
The Annual Review and re-Discovery

All of the Organic Referral material we've covered so far applies to clients and centers-of-influence, new or existing. However, once you embrace the concept of Organic Referrals, retrofitting it into your existing client base can prove to be daunting.

The easiest and most efficient way to bring your current clients into the Organic Referral fold is through the annual review. Over the course of a year or two you can introduce the concepts slowly but surely by integrating them into the annual review agenda.

I'll repeat what you just read at the end of the section of the delivery: "In setting up the annual review, it's important to adhere to the 'no surprises' best practice and ask permission to bring up the topic of referrals. It's polite, courteous and bespeaks professionalism."

With that in mind, what follows is a best-practices agenda for the annual review, which I consider to be the focal event in one's client management system.

Annual review objectives

1. Keep clients satisfied and keep their business on the books.
2. Review the client's holdings and performance and adjust strategy as needed
3. Identify or initiate any "next sale" opportunity for the client or any assets the client controls.
4. Obtain quality prospects.

Time/Place

- Approximately1 hour, preferably in the Advisor's office.

Attendees

- Client, Producer
- Optional: Other household members, client representatives or producer's assistant/paraplanner

Before Meeting

- Review notes from last client meeting.
- Review client holdings and financial goals.
- Prospect/client re-Discovery form (keying off your existing fact-finder) to gather

additional demographics and updates to existing information.

- Client holdings and performance information from Client Relationship Management database and other sources.
- Assemble a list of names to use as prompts for potential referrals (see the Mapping Exercise in Chapter Two, part 4)
- Applications or service forms anticipated for client signature.
- Assemble other documents for use in meeting.

Meeting Checklist

- Greeting and chit-chat. This casual, conversational step is designed to reconnect with the client and uncover life events among important people in the client's world. This is a critical piece in the gathering of Organic Referrals. Life events are events that might unexpectedly happen or are planned such as pregnancy, job change, graduation, illness, moving or retirement (to name but a few). These life events can identify prospects, sales opportunities, and/or personal touches that can be made.

- Uncover any important issues on the client's mind. Record these for addressing when appropriate during the meeting.

- Update demographic information and gather additional details for the database to be used for proactive client contact (hobbies, interests, college affiliation, email, contact preferences). Use the existing fact-finder to record these updates and re-discoveries. As with the discovery period we discussed earlier for new clients, Organic Referrals are served by getting existing clients used to divulging names of people important to their fiscal network and talking about why they were chosen for that role. If you haven't recorded those names before, the annual review is an excellent time to do so.

- Overview of the global/national/local financial environment from the advisor's viewpoint and client's viewpoint. Examine the client's holdings within this broader financial environment. Utilize the iconic image (Chapter Two) to reinforce the work you've done together. This also reemphasizes your value proposition for the Organic Referral process.

- Discuss any recommended changes to holdings.

- Explain the scope of advisory products and services, including anything new. The use of the iconic image assists in this step. This will prevent the classic: "Oh, I didn't know you did that!" downer.

- Identify and plant the seeds for the next step to secure the client's financial future (next opportunity).

- Identify any assets the client controls that might be up for a competitive bid. Here you are trading on knowledge of the client's role in another person's fiscal life.

- Ask how the client feels about the level of service they are receiving from you and your office to determine if they want to make any adjustments.

- As promised in setting up the review, you can now segue into the referral section of the meeting. We reviewed the various components of this: Mapping Exercise, Market Focus List and names generated during the discovery.

- Verbally summarize the key outcomes of the meeting.

After-Meeting

Communicate and/or provide staff the following:

- Demographic and personal information updates and notes for database entry. This includes a reassessed client segmentation rating as a result of the review and scheduling possible personal touches, as in an anticipated graduation or pregnancy due date.
- New prospects/referrals added to the to-do list for scheduling an initial appointment.
- Anticipated sales opportunities recorded for follow-up.
- Client service requests and adjustments to be processed.
- A review of the key points of the meeting so a summary letter and thank-you note is sent for any referrals received.
- Schedule the next contact.

If you don't have a fact-finder and are interested in a one-page summary of information you ought to have about your top tier clients, let me know and I can provide you with my "Client Info-Card." This is a condensed "re-discovery" tool that you can adapt for use with your CRM , database or old-fashioned client files.

Send the request to: practicedoc@gmail.com

Part IV
Organic Referrals and Key Business Partners

Chapter 9
Centers-of-Influence

A popular Organic Referral resource is a dedicated center-of-influence (COI) meeting with the sole purpose of exploring names and contacts.

My definition of a COI is unrestricted to particular professions. Some producers will define COIs as attorneys, CPAs and bankers. While these are certainly part of the mix, many producers find it difficult to find reciprocity with these other professionals.
Consequently, in my book a COI is defined as:

"Anyone with influence in a network and/or market that you are interested in penetrating. They are willing to help you with introductions and insight into the network."

A good example is Paul, an advisor in a community of about 100,000. His primary COI is Bob, a retired engineer he knows through his local church. Bob has been – and still is - involved in all sorts of activities in the community including serving on boards, being politically active, helping with charities, and being active in church offices. He also maintains contacts from his past career as a manager with IBM. In other words, Bob pretty much knows everyone in town and is a COI whose network is the entire community. He is an "unlimited" COI, always generating new contacts.

Paul and Bob sit down every six months or so at the local diner (Bob likes their homemade pies) to review Paul's marketing strategies, Market Focus List and progress on any referrals recently obtained.

When I asked Paul how he brings on board a COI, he responded:

"It's a long process. All of the items you've covered in this booklet need to be explored before a COI will become productive."

Paul took me through Bob's development as a COI over time, reviewing the Organic Referral principles.

Paul examined Bob's answers to the questions posed in Chapter One:

> History: Based on his experience, is there any chance this Bob will give me a referral?

"Bob's previous experience with referrals was somewhat negative. He'd been disillusioned when he and his wife had fallen for a multi-level marketing scheme in the 80's and reluctantly bought into a time-share ski resort that ultimately collapsed. He was, however, grateful for referrals to a real estate agent and a painting service. I'd say Bob was wary but willing to see what I could do. He was happy with the investment strategies I designed for his retirement nest egg, which is now in the distribution phase."

> Psychology: What is Bob thinking when I broach the topic of referrals?

"No doubt it's how I will impact his relationships with others. He's a social animal and runs into people he knows everywhere, it seems. So if I disappoint one of his referrals, it's over for me. He can't hide from them and much as he likes me, his relationship network is more important to him than I am as an individual."

> Reality: Am I even referable in the COI's eyes?

"Bob's a business-casual dress guy all the time. He likes that I wear a tie most days and expects some new jokes and stories when we meet. I've been over to his place for dinner and his wife likes me, so that's a big plus! Evidently, my manners and attitude ring true in his eyes...and I know he can sniff out a phony at first glance."

> Reason: What value do I bring that is sufficiently unique to warrant a referral from Bob?

"I use an iconic piece, like you describe. Mine is a "retirement rainbow" sort of visual that carries through the sales and service systems I've set up. He sees how it's played out in his finances, even through the 2008 debacle. He also sees that it's more comprehensive than what he's been doing with me in retirement and send me all age groups for a 'rainbow review' as he calls it."

Can Bob relate to the Iconic Image in Chapter Two to reinforce your value proposition verbally, visually and interactively?

"Yes, as I just mentioned, he's actually using it as a way of promoting me to others."

How about the implementation of the five best practice steps in Chapter Three with Bob?

✓ No surprises!

"We meet formally a couple times a year and there are no surprises. Bob's very conscious about his role as a center. He's a straight-shooter. If it stops being productive for him, he'll tell me. Hopefully that won't be for a while!"

> ✓ Ensuring Bob knows what you do and how to promote you.

"That iconic rainbow makes all the difference. He does promote me as a comprehensive advisor, not just an investment guy which is what he actually has me doing for him."

> ✓ Ensuring Bob knows you are looking for relationships, not just transactions.

"This is an interesting point. Bob will recommend me for a number of single-needs. Last month he send me a young couple who are just starting out and need some help budgeting, putting some money away and term life insurance. But after that, he will occasionally ask after that young couple. 'Paul, how're the Langs doing?' he'll say. So I know he's keeping the relationship aspects in the back of his mind."

> ✓ Help Bob focus on the referrals you want via a Market Focus List.

"This one we're beyond, actually. For a while, I did prompt him with a list of organizations and profiles that I'd like to prospect. He learned them and now if I do have a specific marketing idea to aim for, I just mention it verbally. I do want to say, though, that I use a focus list with clients on reviews to give them a consistent referral message.

✓ Obtain a personal introduction...and follow through.

"Bob at first would call the referral before I contacted them, usually as we were sitting in the restaurant, leaving voice messages, mostly. But now he gives me permission to use his name as a door-opener. I make it a point to buy the pie and coffee at our meetings and will fill him in on the progress of the referrals. We don't discuss confidential stuff, of course, but generalities."

As Paul succinctly puts it:

"Once a COI likes you, would like to see you succeed and really believes you can provide a value-add to people he knows the gates open up. Until then, it could be like pulling teeth which is unsustainable and why most producers give up on the idea."

Chapter 10
Personal & Professional Networking

As a productive member of society, you interact with people both personally and professionally all the time. A producer who has children may be part of sports leagues, school activities, faith-based organizations and day-care routines. Other producers might be involved in the community through charities, volunteer groups, adult sports, and/or social clubs.

When you are meeting people, the Organic Referral adherent always has an antenna up identifying possible contacts: prospects, potential centers-of-influence, or simply people who might be able to open a door into an organization.

The caveat is that most of these personal networks are important to the producer and the main purpose of being in them is not to solicit business but because he or she wants to help make a difference. Organic Referrals from personal networks come only after you've proven your value to the cause or organization. This could take years. People will eventually seek you out if they know what you do and if you are approachable. Don't hide the value you bring to your clients. Don't be pushy about it, either.

Professional networking groups, however, exist for the purpose of contacts and name-sharing. The major problem, according to many producers I work with, is that many of these opportunities get lost in the shuffle and fall through the cracks. Business cards are collected, put into a manila folder and never acted upon. Names are jotted down on scraps of paper and get lost among the stacks of papers on the desk.

This is a potent source of Organic Referrals being squandered. Consequently, a system should be in place to process these names, including having a person who is accountable and able to debrief you on a daily basis. Usually, this is an ADVOCATE ASSISTANT who is empowered to ask the right questions. Marita, an advocate assistant for Terry in Columbia, SC, recalls the following dialogue she had with her agent:

"Terry, you were out yesterday at two events, one for your son's school and one with the chamber committee on finance. Did you meet anyone who you'd like to establish contact with?"

Terry pulls out a business card and the agenda from the chamber meeting with two names scrawled on it:

"This is the card for a sales rep that I met at school. These two names are from the chamber; one is a consultant and the other is the mayor's contact at the county finance board."

"Great. I'll enter their information into the prospect spreadsheet. How would you like to make first contact with them?"

"I'll call the consultant directly. Let's send an introductory packet to the other two; I'll follow-up with a call."

Marita scheduled the call on Terry's to-do list and prepared the mailings for Terry's signature. She put the mailing follow-up calls onto Terry's to-do list five days out. She also had Terry relate any additional information he had collected about the prospects. Usually, she tells me, it's all in his head and if she doesn't ask for it, it'll never get recorded anywhere.

The best practices around processing a networking lead in a Client Relationship Management program includes:

- Populating the entry with basic information: Getting everything Terry knows about the prospect out of his head and into the CRM;

- Activity scheduling: Adding the desired first contact with the prospect on to the to-do list. Is it by phone, mail, or e-mail?
- Posting outcomes: What were the results of Terry's calls? Are the prospects to be called back? Was there an appointment set? Or should the lead be discarded?
- Identifying next steps based on the conversation: Did Terry agree to send some information? When should he call the client again? Who is the gatekeeper for the prospect (who is in charge of his or her appointment book)?
- Creating a daily database routine ensures that prospects aren't slipping through the cracks. There should be a to-do list that keeps items open until completed. The assistant's job is to keep this list to a workable amount.

As you can see, having a robust CRM is valuable. However, Organic Referrals can be tracked on a number of different tools including Outlook, spreadsheets, One-Cards, notebooks and time-management materials.

Postscript

Organic Referrals is a major part of a financial service practice's growth and profitability.

In my book **How To Build Your Financial Advisory Business And Sell It At A Profit** (McGraw-Hill) I cover the eight business systems that comprise every producer's business. In this booklet we addressed the first four of these systems:
- Client Acquisition,
- Client Management,
- Sales Process, and
- Case Development.

These are the Core Four systems and produce the revenue for the producer. We've explored how referrals can organically be infused into the producer's Core Four systems.

The other four systems are:
- Time Management,
- Communication & Operations,
- Education, and
- Financial Management.

In more subtle ways, Organic Referrals can permeate these Infrastructure systems as well. Once you have established the beachhead of Organic Referrals in your practice – that is, into the Core Four systems - we can work together to maximize the concept with your team and attain a truly *inter*dependent practice:

You, your internal team, your clients and your external team, all speaking the same language and attracting high-quality Organic Referrals on an ongoing basis!

Send me your thoughts, stories, ideas, experiences, problems and reactions to this Organic Referral material. All of my best-practice research is a work-in-progress and I'd be happy to share your successes and challenges with other producers.

Al Depman
Rochester, MN
507-216-4641
practicedoc@gmail.com

January, 2012